火	火	火	火	火	火	火	火
道	陰	陽	水	火	土	金	木
33	34	35	36	37	38	39	40
fire ✦ Tao	fire ✦ Yin	fire ✦ Yang	fire ✦ Water	fire ✦ fire	fire ✦ Earth	fire ✦ Metal	fire ✦ Wood
(page 48)	(page 49)	(page 50)	(page 51)	(page 52)	(page 53)	(page 54)	(page 55)

土	土	土	土	土	土	土	土
道	陰	陽	水	火	土	金	木
41	42	43	44	45	46	47	48
Earth ✦ Tao	Earth ✦ Yin	Earth ✦ Yang	Earth ✦ Water	Earth ✦ fire	Earth ✦ Earth	Earth ✦ Metal	Earth ✦ Wood
(page 56)	(page 57)	(page 58)	(page 59)	(page 60)	(page 61)	(page 62)	(page 63)

金	金	金	金	金	金	金	金
道	陰	陽	水	火	土	金	木
49	50	51	52	53	54	55	56
Metal ✦ Tao	Metal ✦ Yin	Metal ✦ Yang	Metal ✦ Water	Metal ✦ fire	Metal ✦ Earth	Metal ✦ Metal	Metal ✦ Wood
(page 64)	(page 65)	(page 66)	(page 67)	(page 68)	(page 69)	(page 70)	(page 71)

木	木	木	木	木	木	木	木
道	陰	陽	水	火	土	金	木
57	58	59	60	61	62	63	64
Wood ✦ Tao	Wood ✦ Yin	Wood ✦ Yang	Wood ✦ Water	Wood ✦ fire	Wood ✦ Earth	Wood ✦ Metal	Wood ✦ Wood
(page 72)	(page 73)	(page 74)	(page 75)	(page 76)	(page 77)	(page 78)	(page 79)

TAO

道

STONES

Chinese meditations for every day

TAO

STONES

ZHAO XIAOMIN
and
MARTIN PALMER

FRIEDMAN/FAIRFAX

This edition published by the Michael Friedman Publishing
Group, Inc. by arrangement with Eddison Sadd Editions.

ISBN 1-58663-708-8

2002 Friedman/Fairfax

10 9 8 7 6 5 4 3 2 1

For bulk purchases and special sales, please contact:
Michael Friedman Publishing Group, Inc.
Attention: Sales Department
230 Fifth Avenue, Suite 700
New York, NY 10001
Tel: 212/685-6610
Fax: 212/685-3916

Visit our website:
www.metrobooks.com

EDDISON • SADD EDITIONS LIMITED
St Chad's House
148 King's Cross Road
London, WC1X 9DH

Phototypeset in Braganza, Frutiger and Venetian using
QuarkXPress on Apple Macintosh
Origination by Bright Arts, Singapore
Printed by Hung Hing Offset Printing Co. Ltd., China

Contents

Introduction

The actual remains are tiny, fragile and, at first sight, appear insignificant. They lie in a museum, close to the ancient Chinese city of Xian. How they have managed to survive for over 5,000 years is a miracle itself, for the fragments are made of pottery and lay buried and unknown for millennia ...

It was in the 1950s that the Neolithic village of Banpo was unearthed, one of the most complete examples of such an early Chinese settlement. Among the finds were the usual kinds of materials and artefacts: pots, bone implements, stone axes and the remains of the huts. The decorations on the pots are astonishingly beautiful, made up of complex – almost abstract – designs of fish, birds, and even human faces.

Yet, exciting as these are, perhaps the most challenging and unexpected discoveries would have gone unnoticed if it had not been for sharp-eyed archaeologists. On such sites, masses of bits of broken pottery are always uncovered. But, uniquely at this site, pieces were found on which simple and, as yet, unexplained signs were engraved, cut deep into the fragments. It is clear that they are words or characters and, as such, form the earliest example of symbolic written language ever found in China. But why were they each inscribed on separate pieces of pottery, all roughly the same size – about one inch across? The answer lies in divination.

THE WISDOM OF CHANCE

It seems that these earliest words of Chinese formed part of an ancient divinatory system: the characters would all be put together into a pot, and the fortune-teller would then ask the deities a question. One or two (or possibly more) of the inscribed pieces would then be drawn from the pot at random, and the signs interpreted to give a reading – a response from the deities to the question asked.

This is the essence of Chinese wisdom or divination: it is essentially about chance. Those looking for a system which will tell you exactly what to do will not find it, for that is not how the Chinese systems work. Chinese philosophy has always stressed that while certain things in life are fixed – when and where you are born, for example – the rest of life is for you to determine. In the end, you can become whom you wish, if you truly decide to be a certain kind of person. This is reflected in the famous ancient Chinese Examination System, the structure of which meant that, in theory, even the poorest child from a remote part of China, could, through hard work, become prime minister.

The heart of Chinese divination is the seeking of wisdom. To do this you need to abandon all attempts at logic and reason and instead allow the greater wisdom of the Tao – of Nature itself – to break through. This happens when you allow chance to dictate the guidance you need. The 5,000-year-old fragments of pottery are examples of allowing random choice to dictate the reading. Today, instead of pulling bits of marked pottery from a pot, many Chinese will just open a book of poems at random and be guided by the verses they encounter. Both systems are as good as each other, for in the end what this randomness, this chance, allows is for a wisdom greater than our own to 'break in' upon us, and thus help us to explore anew the issues which concern or excite us, and upon which we feel the need for guidance.

THE MEDITATION STONES

Here, these two systems have been brought together in the form of meditation stones. The eight characters used on the stones are, in essence, a distillation of Chinese philosophical wisdom.

The first three characters embody the cosmos: Tao is the ultimate force, or nature, of existence, while yin and yang are the two primal forces of the universe. Total opposites, yin is female, wet, cold, winter, while yang is male, dry, hot, summer. Locked in perpetual struggle, they contain the seed of each other within them – thus winter gives way to summer and summer gives way to winter. This dynamic is what keeps the world spinning.

The remaining five characters are the five elements of Chinese philosophy. These elements are the stuff of this world – Water, Fire, Wood, Metal and Earth. This fusion of the cosmic three and the elemental five forces brings to bear the most fundamental aspects of Chinese thought to provide a doorway into wisdom and perception, and offer guidance for our lives today.

PART ONE

The Way of the Tao

The character for 'Tao' in Chinese is one you will see in any town or city, for it simply means 'road' or 'street'. Thus 'Beijing Tao' translates as 'Beijing Road'. Yet, while it has this straightforward meaning, over the millennia of Chinese history this simple word has come to be the most mysterious and spiritually charged of all Chinese characters – so mysterious that it defies description, as Lao Tzu wrote in the Taoist classic, *Tao Te Ching*, over 2,000 years ago:

> *The Tao that can be talked about is not the true Tao.*
> *The name that can be named is not the eternal Name.*

What can have happened to a word meaning 'road' to turn it into something so astonishingly powerful?

THE EVOLUTION OF TAO

The Tao, with its meaning of 'path', 'way' or 'road', was being used as a term for the spiritual or moral pathway as early as 2,500 years ago. Confucius, the great scholar sage of China, spoke of the Tao as the moral Way of the Universe – a kind of underlying moral force which dictated how the universe operated. For him, the Tao was the natural way to behave:

> *What Heaven has given is called the law of Nature.*
> *To follow this natural way is to follow the Tao [Way].*
> *To nurture this Tao is called learning.*
> *The Tao must not be left, even for a moment.*
> *If it could be left, then it would not be the Tao.*
>
> THE DOCTRINE OF THE MEAN

It is the forerunners of Taoism, the great sages like Lao Tzu (sixth century BCE) and Chuang Tzu (fourth century BCE), who took this moral code and elevated it into a spiritual insight – an understanding and relationship with the Origin of the Origin, the Tao. As Chuang Tzu wrote:

The great Way is not named,
The great disagreement is unspoken,
Great benevolence is not benevolent,
Great modesty is not humble,
Great courage is not violent.
The Tao that is clear is not the Tao,
Speech which enables argument is not worthy,
Benevolence which is ever present does not achieve its goal,
Modesty flouted, fails,
Courage that is violent is pointless.

CHAPTER 2, THE CHUANG TZU

In Taoist cosmology, the Tao is that from which all flows. It is beautifully summed up by Lao Tzu in the *Tao Te Ching*, in what is, in effect, the 'Creed of Taoism'. The 'Two' Lao Tzu cites are yin and yang, the opposing forces of the universe through whose cosmic struggle to overcome one another the dynamism of the universe is generated. The 'Three' are Heaven, which is yang, Earth, which is yin, and Humanity, which holds both in balance. Ch'i is the breath of Tao, the life-force which enlivens all existence — including the five elements.

The Creed of Taoism

The Tao is the Origin of the One,
The One gives birth to the Two;
The Two give birth to the Three.
The Three give birth to every living thing.
All things are held in yin and carry yang:
And they are held together by the ch'i of teeming energy.

CHAPTER 42, TAO TE CHING

Taoist cosmology absorbed the five elements of classical Chinese philosophy within the wider development of the Tao as the ultimate force. In using these eight key characters, the system of meditation stones presented here brings together the core of the Chinese world-view and, through it, seeks to emphasize the necessity of allowing the originality and universalism of the Tao to break through our somewhat pitiful human attempts to work out, for ourselves, what the world is all about.

GOING WITH THE FLOW

Listening to the Tao is listening to the heartbeat of the world, of the universe, and it is about learning to be still, to be humble and to go with the flow of nature ...

> *The Tao moves in every direction at once —*
> *Its essence is fluid and yielding.*
> *It is the maker of everything under the sun:*
> *And everything comes out of nothing.*
>
> CHAPTER 40, TAO TE CHING

The Tao is not a god, or God. The Tao is the fundamental nature of all life, and the origin of all that life. It has neither personality nor emotion. It just is. The role of the meditation stones is to put you in direct touch with this cosmic force, and to see if, in doing so, you can begin to live more in accordance with the natural ebb and flow of life. Many of us struggle to make of life that which we believe it should be. The stones, in the true spirit of Taoism, ask you to cease from this struggle, and instead to allow the Tao to guide you along paths, ways — along the Tao that is, in fact, the very flow of life itself.

─────────────── ೞ ───────────────

Using the Meditation Stones

The eight characters which form the basis of the meditation stones themselves embody the very heart of Chinese spirituality and philosophy. In Chinese belief, the written character has a mystical, almost magical power both in and of itself. In Taoism, written characters *are* actually magical; they embody and hold the very forces they describe. Taoist charms, for example, use a form of calligraphy which turns the character into a picture of the very thing it is describing. This symbolic, pictorial power lies at the heart of the Chinese character, for they originated in shamanic oracles and the inspection of cracks in oracle bones, which were 'read' to provide answers to questions. In other words, pictures are the origin of Chinese characters, and this origin still shapes – both literally and spiritually – their significance today.

Thus in looking at a character you are, to some degree, looking at that which the character actually describes or defines, or that which concerns the actual entity. For example, the character for Wood is a symbolic tree *(see page 13)*: you can see the actual trunk and branches in its shape. Other characters are more complex. The one for yang, for instance *(see page 12)*, symbolizes – through use of the symbol of the sun – the sunny side of a mountain or hill (in other words, the hot or warm side).

Chinese characters, because they both represent and present the concept that they embody, have an element of that concept within them. Writing them evokes the very forces that they represent.

THE EIGHT CHARACTERS

Tao

We have already explored the character of Tao in detail in Part One. In essence, it is the ultimate force of the universe, the Origin of the Origin. Its roots lie in the word for 'road' or 'path', and this came to symbolize, or stand for, the True Path, the real Way of life.

Yin

Yin represents the female, the intuitive, winter and autumn, the cold and wet nature of life. It stands in complete contrast to yang. But it is important to stress that neither yin nor yang is 'good' or 'bad'. They simply *are*. They are not divine forces so much as the building blocks of life itself, for it is through their dynamic interaction that life is generated and the life-force kept spinning.

Yang

Yang represents the male, the instructive, summer and spring, the hot and dry nature of existence. It is often seen as the dominant force in popular mythology. Thus, for example, the sun is yang while the moon is yin and, because of the perceived greater power of the sun, yang is thought to be more powerful. This is not the case; both yin and yang are equally balanced in their influences. And, of course, the ultimate truth of both yin and yang is that, as the symbol shows, each contains a speck of the other within it, and thus the seed for the growth of the opposite force. So, winter is deepest yin, but has within it the seed of spring, which is yang. Likewise, summer is deepest yang, but contains within it the seed of autumn, which brings yin round again.

THE FIVE ELEMENTS

In Greek and early Buddhist thought, there were only four elements: Earth, Fire, Air and Water. The Chinese development of the five elements (first written down in the fourth century BCE) is unique, and seems to have arisen from the experimental nature of early Chinese religion, which was driven by the quest for the Pill of Immortality. It was believed that if the right concoction of materials was prepared in the correct way, a pill bestowing long life – or even the ability to live forever – could be manufactured. Some emperors, such as the First Emperor (221–209 BCE), spent unbelievable sums of money in pursuit of this goal, and this funded religious explorers to investigate all kinds of strange mixtures and to test the properties – indeed, the very elements of nature – in search for this elusive pill. Thus the five elements of Water, Fire, Earth, Metal and Wood were born – the five building blocks of the physical world.

Water

Water is the first of the five elements and is, of course, fundamental to life. No water, no life. Our bodies are some 75–80 per cent water. Water was also seen in most cosmologies as the first element in existence.

Fire

Fire is the opposite of water. It destroys, yet from the ashes comes new life. Fire is thus both a fierce, painful force – the written character derives from a picture of a burning branch – and a force which warms, with which we can cook, and which helps humanity to clear land through the burning of scrubland or forests.

Earth

Earth literally means the physical substance of the earth but also, to a lesser extent, the earth itself. It is the stuff of which all life is made, for the Chinese creation stories are based on a similar notion to that in the Bible: that the sentient world was moulded from the earth itself.

Metal

Metal is the first of the 'unusual' elements, normally subsumed under the earth from which it comes. The inclusion of metal in the Chinese list is indicative of the experimental and proto-scientific basis of early Chinese society. The recognition of the creation of metal illustrates a society which has done more than just observe what lies around. Metal is the element of transformation.

Wood

Wood is the other unusual element here, in that it does not usually feature in lists of the elements. In Chinese thought, wood is that which fuels fire and helps create earth itself. Wood also symbolizes the flexibility of the elements, since wood (in the form of trees) is able to bend in the wind and thus spring back even when great storms sweep over it.

In combining these five elements with the three cosmic forces of Tao, yin and yang, we bring together the very forces of nature to help you find your place within the universe.

HOW TO USE THE MEDITATION STONES

The idea of the meditation stones is very simple. They offer a process of reflection, providing a mechanism for randomness and calm by inviting you to stop, prepare yourself, and allow the moment of chance to occur. By abandoning all attempts to control your destiny, manipulate the world or even divine what is to be, you thus allow random chance to give you two characters — characters which direct you to a reading on which you can then reflect for the day.

There are two sets of eight stones in this pack, each set containing the eight key characters. The sets would traditionally be kept separate for reading purposes, and thus are differentiated here by colour — one black, one grey — to help you when you make your reading (there is no significance in the colours themselves).

MAKING A READING

Before you begin, you need to put the two sets of stones into the cloth bag provided. The bag is divided into two compartments: place the grey set in one compartment, and the black set into the other. Your meditation stones are now ready for use. Follow the simple steps below to find a reading, or meditation.

1 Preparation First, try to calm your mind in order to be receptive to what comes. If there is a question or concern that is foremost in your thoughts, you may choose to bring this to mind. But remember: this is not about getting answers, but about seeking wisdom or insights on which you can reflect, and from which you might be better able to find the answers for yourself. It is a form of meditation.

2 Selecting your stones Pull a stone from one compartment of the bag (it doesn't matter which colour you pick first). Check the character against those shown on pages 11–13 and write down which one it is. Then pull a stone from the other compartment and note this down. You should always end up with one stone of each colour. Make sure you note down the characters in the order that you picked them, as this plays a role in the next step.

3 Finding your reading The order of your characters directs you to a specific combination, which gives you your reading. You can check the combination in the visual index found at the front and back of the book (once you become more familiar with the stones, you will be able to identify your combination based on the characters alone). For example, say you draw Tao black, followed by Fire grey. This gives you TAO as your first character and FIRE as your second. When you check the index, you see that Tao/Fire is reading number 5; you can then turn to the relevant page in the book for your reading. Or, say you pick Earth grey, then Metal black. This gives you Earth/Metal, which is reading number 47. (NOTE: If both stones you pick have the same character, then there is only one combination, so the order is not relevant.)

THE MEDITATIONS

There are sixty-four readings altogether, featured on the following pages. Each reading consists of a proverb, poem and meditation. Study the proverb first: this will give you a feel for the meditation. The poem then takes you to an astonishing level. Each poem has come from the oldest known book of Chinese poetry, the *Shih Ching*. Compiled between the ninth and fifth centuries BCE, it contains much earlier material, from around 1500 to 1000 BCE. These oracles, poems and prayers have served the Chinese for millennia, and contain great wisdom and beauty. The meditation given with each reading offers a contemporary reflection, drawing upon the insights, symbols and concepts within the poem, clarifying the message.

You should also look at the combination of characters you have chosen. The interrelationship between them can itself often provide insights, as is occasionally highlighted in the meditation.

By taking a reading at the beginning of each day, the Voice of the Tao will help you find your own way through the complexities of contemporary life, casting a new light on issues that concern you, or simply suggesting a meditational thought to hold in your mind. You may even wish to carry the two stones with you through the day: this is believed to be auspicious, and it is thought that touching them can help keep you rooted in both their physical solidity and their spiritual wisdom. Calmed by your meditation, you can feel part of a greater purpose: the flow of the Tao through all life.

Tao ❖ Tao

PROVERB
The best tactic of all is running away.

I leave by the north gate
My grief overcomes me
I am dead broke and hungry
Yet no one hears my cries.
Well, the worst has happened
No doubt it was fate
So why bother talking about it?

MEDITATION
The north gate symbolizes the direction of difficulties. Do not try to resist what has already happened – instead, look to the future. You have survived. Celebrate that, and draw strength for the better days to come.

1

Tao ❖ Yin

PROVERB

You can't expect both ends of a sugar cane to be
equally sweet.

See the little stars
Shrinking in the eastern night?
Shrinking, as we walk through dark
While it is still night in the palace
Burdened with cover and sheet
Ah! our fates are not equal.

MEDITATION

Life is not fair – and to expect that it should be is
foolishness. Learn to see the world more realistically, and
enjoy that which comes your way. Envy at the success of
others can be damaging.

2

Tao ❖ Yang

道
陽

PROVERB

When a leopard dies, he leaves his skin; when a man dies, he leaves his reputation.

See the foul rat? He has skin.
A man without pride,
A man without pride,
Why is he living? Why doesn't he die?

See the foul rat? He has legs.
A man without custom,
A man without custom,
He'd better die soon.

MEDITATION

What you do lives on. As Shakespeare says, 'The good that a man does, dies with him; the ill lives on.' Look to what you do and why you do it. Think of how the future will judge you.

Tao ❖ Water

PROVERB

Shed no tears till you see the coffin.

The ducks are sleeping on the island
The dead man is calm and peaceful
His food is hot and tasty
His drink is spicy and warm
The dead man drinks quietly.
The blessings come from Heaven.

MEDITATION

All things come at the appointed time. Do not try to rush
that which requires time to mature. Make your preparations
as the mourners do for their dead. It is only in the fullness
of time, however, that all will come to pass, and your patience
will be rewarded by Heaven.

4

Tao ✦ fire

PROVERB

Use power against power, force against force.

Kneel down, kneel down!
Heaven sees and knows all!
It watches us, day in, day out
I, a mere stripling,
Am not respectful or wise
But as the days go by
I listen to the bright shining ones.
O brightness, O light,
Show me the right way,
Show me the ways of power.

MEDITATION

There are two great forces here: Tao, The Way, and Fire, great destroyer but also bringer of warmth and power. You have great potential but you need to find the right guide – the Tao – and harness the forces in such a way as to do what is right and proper. If you do, then the future can be a bright one.

5

Tao ✦ Earth

PROVERB

Don't worry about going slowly; start panicking when you stop.

How few of us are left!
Why do we not retreat?
Were it not for the king's politics,
Why would we be stuck in the mud?

MEDITATION

Following false advice, even when it comes from the top, leads to troubles. Just as the soldiers of the past regretted the leadership of poor kings, so you should examine with care the advice you are given – including this advice!

6

Tao ✦ Metal

道
金

PROVERB

A tiger won't return to prey it didn't kill.

Don't chase the big chariot
You'll only choke on dust
Don't think about the world's pain
You'll only make yourself miserable.

Don't chase the big chariot
You'll be blinded with dust
Don't think about the world's pain
Or you will never escape from despair.

MEDITATION

The Way can be hard, just like metal. It commands restraint and a recognition of appropriateness. Be modest. Do not pretend to be a tiger, or to follow the ways of the great, chasing the king's chariot. Do not think you can solve all the world's problems. Be hard on yourself and exercise restraint and due humility.

7

Tao ◆ Wood

PROVERB

A king's favour is like the wind; his anger is like lightning.

The willow is very leafy
But I wouldn't rest under it.
The king is very bright
Don't get too close to him!
Question his words
And he'll kill you on the spot.

MEDITATION

There is a right way to grow – just as a tree does, obeying the law of Tao. Around you, life swirls and trembles. It can seem so exciting, but the dangers are great. Be like the willow, which bends when the wind blows, and so survives.

8

Yin ❖ Tao

陰
道

PROVERB

You can't get a tiger cub without going into his
mother's den.

The one who gave birth to us
This was our mother.
How did she do this?
She prayed and she sacrificed
To cure her barrenness
And she trod on the giant's tracks
Proved herself, and had her desire.

MEDITATION

This is a poem in praise of loving determination. To be
barren in ancient China, as in much of the ancient world,
was considered a disgrace. However, using all means possible
– including prayer and magic – the woman succeeds. That
which is really worthwhile involves effort and even sacrifice.

Yin ❖ Yin

PROVERB

When the ear doesn't listen, the heart escapes pain.

In sickness, in health, in death as in life,
This is the oath I swear to you always.
I take your hand in mine,
To show we will grow old together.

I weep for those oaths,
Which have not lasted even one lifetime.
I weep for our trust,
You could not even trust me.

MEDITATION

If you vow, if you promise, if you trust, do so sincerely.
There is no pain of the heart so great as a broken heart,
shattered by betrayal. It breaks not only the heart of the
betrayed, but also that of the betrayer. Hold fast to truth.

10

Yin ✦ Yang

PROVERB

If a son is ignorant, it's his father's fault.

The herbs grow thick;
Not healing herbs, but wormwood.
I weep for my father and mother.
I weep for their effort in raising me.
'That the cup should be empty
Humiliates the jar.'
Better to have died long ago
Than to live like a commoner!

My father bred me
My mother fed me,
Led me, taught me
Raised me, kept me
Watched me, tended me
At every point helped me.
I would give them good in return
It is fate's fault, not mine!

陰
陽

MEDITATION

If you are not as you wish, look within. You can blame others,
but only you can use what you have been given. Ignorance
can be the fault of others, but if you have been nurtured
and still fail, you are like the herbs which only produce poison.
The balance between yin and yang is yours to resolve.

Yin ✦ Water

PROVERB

A toad can be a better husband than a tiger.

The terrace shines clear
But the water runs murky
She sought a fine husband;
Found only a filthy toad.

We spread the fish-nets;
A wild goose was caught there.
She sought a lovely man,
But got this hop-toad.

MEDITATION

Two yin forces mean you may not have the exact balance in life you dream of, but do not despise what you have. Your dream could have become a nightmare – the tiger of the proverb. Instead, you have had to settle for slightly less, but in the long run the true worth of a person is not on the outside, or in their apparent position or power, but rather on the inside, in the depth of their soul.

12

Yin ✦ fire

PROVERB

Lift the heart of a friend by writing his name on a
dragon's wings.

My lord burns for me
In his left hand he grasps a flute
With his right he beckons to me
Oh, such joy!

My lord is free and happy
In his left hand he holds a dancing feather
With his right he calls me to him
Oh, such joy!

陰
火

MEDITATION

Celebrate all that is good, for you are blessed. Not with great
wealth of the material kind but by friendships worthy of the
name; by love of the kind many long for, and by the ability
to recognize the good and also the potential that
surrounds you. Enjoy.

13

Yin ✷ Earth

PROVERB

Heaven gives you a soul; the earth will give you your grave.

Alive, they could never be together
But in death they slept in the same earth.
'You thought I had broken my promise,
But I was as true as the sun and stars.'

MEDITATION

Truth, like death, cannot be avoided.
When things seem to be falling apart,
stand firm and true, just as yin and
earth are one: yin is Earth, yang is
Heaven. This poem reminds you that
you will ultimately find the truth and
know who has been true to you
throughout.

陰
土

14

Yin ✦ Metal

PROVERB

Don't butcher the donkey once he's done his job on the mill.

Ah, so sweet and pretty are the songbirds,
Resting on the side of the hill there.
The way is long; my weapons are heavy;
I am exhausted; no good will come of this.

陰金

MEDITATION

Perhaps, this poem is saying, you should reflect upon what you are doing. Listen to the birds rather than striving after victory. As Christ said, 'Look at the Lilies of the Valley which neither spin nor sow; yet God clothes them.' This is the heart of this poem. Likewise, when you are successful, do not despise or ignore those around you who made it possible. Learn to reflect, relax and trust.

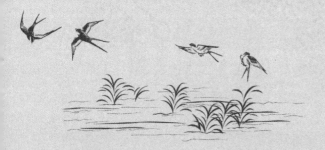

Yin ◆ Wood

PROVERB

A dog won't abandon a poor master; a son won't desert an
ugly mother.

When the soft south wind
Blows into the thorn-bushes
It full freshens their heart
But our mother had only care.

The gentle south wind
Blows on the thorn-wood
Our mother was good and wise
But none of us are any use.

MEDITATION

Do you honour those who support you? The Wood element
symbolizes growth, but growth must be nurtured; the yin is
the female, nurturing, earthly and motherly dimension. Do
you really allow this to shape how you develop, how you
grow? If not, then look again at your roots: your family, your
friends, those who care for you because of who you are, not
what you are. Be nourished and, in return, grow true and tall
like the poplar tree or bamboo.

16

Yang ◆ Tao

陽
道

PROVERB

When you have two coins left, buy bread with one and a lily
with the other.

What flower is not broken?
What hour do we not march?
What man is not seized
To guard the Empire's borders?

What plant is not withered?
What man is not torn from his wife?
Weep for us soldiers,
Treated as though we were not men at all!

MEDITATION

Life is fleeting. Our destinies are, in part, for us to shape,
but external forces also make or break us. This sad but
beautiful poem speaks from feudal China, where the emperor
could order men to war as he wished. The proverb thus
urges us to enjoy each day by ensuring that we have
not just the necessities but that we also delight in the
ordinary wonders of everyday life: flowers, our families –
all that we take for granted. Find the Tao that makes
each day special.

Yang ✦ Yin

PROVERB

Do not employ handsome servants, or pretty maids.

I went to the east hills,
Bore my sword, slept under my cart.
Too many years away,
And when I came back
How the rain poured down!
'The birds are flying
See the glint of their wing!'
A girl is getting married
Her horses are white and bay,
And her mother has tied her girdle.
All the rites and customs are there.
This new marriage is very pretty
But what about the old one?

MEDITATION

Balance is the essence of yang and yin. But it does
not come easily. It has to be maintained. In Chinese
philosophy it is our role to balance yang and yin:
Heaven and Earth. This is done through correct
behaviour and great rituals. For most of us, however,
keeping this balance is also needed in relationships, the most
fundamental of which are those between partners, and
parents and their children. The proverb warns that it is easy
to be distracted from keeping this personal yang/yin balance.

18

Yang ✦ Yang

陽
陽

PROVERB

Soldiers to a minister are like ants to a boy.

Minister of War,
We are the king's sharp claws
Why do you dip us in misery,
With no time to rest or halt?

Minister of War,
We are the king's fierce teeth
Why do you dip us in misery,
When our mothers lack food?

MEDITATION

These words warn against violence, against machismo and against arrogance. Yang is the force of fire and the masculine. The two together can be very powerful but also very dangerous. Harness these forces or, like the soldiers of the poem and proverb, your anger, your strength, will be used by others who care little for you in reality. Be controlling, not controlled.

Yang ❖ Water

PROVERB

Kill the chicken before the monkey.

Don't teach monkeys to climb —
Or pour water onto wet plaster.
This is known already to all,
Why bother to repeat things?

The snow may be thick-fallen
But when sunshine comes, it melts.
Yet none of you, my lords,
Will offer your retirement.

陽
水

MEDITATION

Don't do what everyone else has already done! This is the
message behind this delightful, teasing poem. If you keep
redoing what has already been done perfectly well
before, you will be wasting your time. Choose
wisely how to act — as the proverb says. Much of
what we do is as irrelevant as the snow — beautiful
to see, but not permanent.

20

Yang ◆ Fire

PROVERB

A long night brings powerful dreams.

Sleep on the rush-mats
Sleep slow and happily
He sleeps, he wakes,
He gives out his dreams.
What did you dream of?
Black bears and brown,
Serpents and snakes.

Black bears and brown,
You will bear a boy
Serpents and snakes,
A girl will come later.

MEDITATION

This combination speaks of powerful, elemental forces. The poem – one of the oldest-known Chinese poems – is rooted in shamanism (the two great manifestations of the spirit world are the bear and snake). As the proverb reveals, this is forceful stuff. You have the power to undertake things. You need to understand the forces you play with, and respect them. Perhaps you are able to play some small but significant role in furthering the aims of God – of the spiritual world. Zoroastrianism (which believes that in the struggle against evil and ignorance, God needs us to do what is right for God to have the power to overcome evil) is what lies at the heart of this message.

Yang • Earth

PROVERB

Virtue can't live alone; neighbours will spring up around it.

Dark plains soil, good for crops,
The plants there sweet as cakes.
We grow here, we meet to govern,
The tortoise-omens are cast.
Stop here, then, stop here,
Build your houses in this place.

MEDITATION

This poem is famous because it tells us how decisions were made in ancient China. When a momentous decision was needed – such as where a wandering people should settle – the gods were asked their advice through a strange divination process using cracks in tortoise-shell. So this poem advises you to turn to Heaven, to God, and go humbly in prayer, meditation and quiet – hear in your heart what is right to do. The proverb indicates that those who build their actions on such a foundation will find they are supported by others attracted to the virtues and values thus displayed.

22

Yang ◆ Metal

陽金

PROVERB

A monkey in yellow robes still has hairy cheeks and a
dirty behind.

That fine man —
Bears a pike and spear
That fine lord —
Polished greaves and red head-band!

The pelican sits on the bridge.
It has not dipped in the water.
That fine gentleman
Has no right to those clothes.

MEDITATION

You can almost hear the clash of yang and Metal — two
forces of strength which find it hard to co-exist. This strange
poem and humorous proverb are the Chinese version of *The
Emperor's New Clothes*. Do not be deceived by external
appearances: look beneath to see the truth.

23

Yang ◆ Wood

PROVERB

The rabbit always has three entrances to its den.

The rabbit nets are hammered in
Spread across the pathways.
Brave and firm are our soldiers
Heart and belly of our lord.

MEDITATION

Wood is yin, thus giving a yin/yang combination. Therefore
this poem and proverb are about recognizing difference and
taking care. At one level the poem seems to say the strong,
young soldiers are invincible compared to the rabbits. But the
proverb balances this. To escape or avoid trouble, you do not
have to go at it headlong. The *Tao Te Ching*, the great classic
book of Taoism, says be like water confronted with a rock.
Go round it, under it and pass on, leaving the solid
young rock far behind.

24

Water ✦ Tao

PROVERB

No waves without the wind.

The reed boat tosses on the waters
Floating, buffeted by waves
My heart is chaos; I cannot sleep
Yet my grief stays secret;
I have wine, all I need,
For play, for fun and games.

But my heart is no mirror
Reflecting what others want.
I have many brothers,
And cannot be kidnapped
But when I appealed to them
They were angry with me.

MEDITATION

Who is your real friend? Who is the pillar against which to rest? Who is the safe haven when life tosses you about? Find them, this poem says. Just as the Prodigal Son, in the story told by Jesus, learned the hard way who were his fair-weather friends and who really loved him, so you need to do the same.

25

Water ❖ Yin

PROVERB

No matter how many times a river divides, it still ends up
in the sea.

The Kiang splits and joins again
Our lady went to be wed
And didn't take her maids.
She wouldn't take us!
But afterwards — oh, she was sorry.

MEDITATION

You can dodge, twist, turn and hide, but in the end you
will have to face the truth. This wonderfully sharp poem —
what a final line! — puts this very bluntly. The proverb does
so more gently. Life does flow to its end. The question is
whether you can understand that and act accordingly.
Live each day as if it were your last, the Bible says.

26

Water ✦ Yang

PROVERB

Dream different dreams on the same bed.

Foam sprays from the water
Splashing the white rocks
I hear that you are betrothed;
I dare not look on your face.

水
陽

MEDITATION

What I want may not be what you want. Life is not always
that easy. Listen to what the other person desires, dreams of,
hopes for. It may not accord with your own hopes or dreams;
nevertheless, listen, respect and honour the other.

Water ✦ Water

PROVERB

The first glass moistened my lips; the second banished my
loneliness; the third sharpened my inspiration; the fourth
expelled all my troubles; the fifth cleansed every part of my
soul; the sixth made me kin to the immortals; the seventh –
I can take no more!

Fish in the basket!
Mud-fish and tench.
Our host has good wine
In a great store.

Fish in the basket!
Flat-backed and carp.
Our host has good wine
More than enough.

MEDITATION

There is a long and honourable tradition of drunken poets in
China! It is also likely that the ancient shamans, from whose
utterances some of the poems of the ancient book of poetry
arise, used alcohol to assist their trances. The proverb will
make sense to anyone who has drunk deep! Enjoy life;
party, celebrate – but don't make the mistake of
thinking that you really can become an immortal
this way. Real life is not about losing yourself in
indulgence, but finding yourself through time and patience.

28

Water ✦ fire

水火

PROVERB

Stay still in a moment of rage; escape a hundred days
of sorrow.

The duke has gone hunting
Riding in his chariot
Taking the reins like ribbons
The horses moving like dancers —
He is on the wet ground
As the fire springs out
Strong-armed, he takes the tiger
And kneels to his lord.
Beware of such play, duke!
You can only get hurt.

MEDITATION

Adventure and excitement — rage and fury. All powerful
emotions. Yet they can lead to actions and dangers which
cannot easily be undone. The poem is full of symbols
of danger, excitement and threat, but the two elements
are yin and yang in nature. Control the fire with the
calm water and you may be able to achieve the
balance necessary.

Water • Earth

PROVERB
A thousand things can be said without speaking.

Creeping grass growing in the wild,
Heavy loaded with dew.
There was a lovely man there,
Clear-eyed, beautiful, fine headed.
We met together by chance
And all my desire was satisfied.

MEDITATION
Sometimes all just simply falls into place, just as water brings life from the earth. Enjoy, relax – this is no time for worries.

30

Water ◆ Metal

水
金

PROVERB

Be as careful in choosing pleasures as in avoiding disasters.

Those who go against Heaven
Sink to ruin together
As sure as the water runs from a spring.
Rise early, sleep late
Shine and sweep your floor
Set a fine example to others.
Keep your chariots and horses in order,
Your bows, arrows, other such weapons
Pulled taut, ready for war.

MEDITATION

The Tao – the Way – is the true path or course of nature.
In ancient China this was also expressed as the Way of
Heaven – the Heavenly Tao. This has a more moral, ethical
dimension to it than the Tao, which has a spiritual
connotation. So look to the moral and ethical basis
of your life and follow the Tao of Heaven.

31

Water ✦ Wood

PROVERB

There are always ears on the far side of any wall.

My heart is no stone
You cannot roll it
My heart is no mat
You cannot fold it away
I have performed all the rites —
More than you could number!

Oh, sun, ah, moon
Why have you dimmed?
Sadness clings to me
Like an unwashed dress
In the still night I think of it
Longing to leap up and fly away.

MEDITATION

The ancient poems of China, like the ancient poems of Egypt or Israel, as found in the Psalms, are often deeply moving. The pain and sorrow of those betrayed or hurt echoes down the millennia. The poems speak directly to us, person to person, despite the untold centuries between. They ask us to reflect on the eternal difficulty of living, loving, longing and hoping. Hold this poem in your mind and think of all those who today feel the same — perhaps even you yourself, or someone close to you.

32

fire ❖ Tao

PROVERB

The longer the night lasts, the more ghosts will come.

The temple is still for the ghosts
The helpers stand silent in awe
The nobles who assist the dead
Have been purified and purged.

Heaven displays its answering spirits
They flit through the temple so fast
As bright and glorious as the sun
Showing no disdain for we mortals.

MEDITATION

The past is not a foreign country, as some would say – it
is what helps us shape our present life and our future.
But China has always taught – despite the often-
seeming fatalism of Buddhism – that we are
ultimately in control of how we use what has
happened to us to determine our future. This poem
and proverb ask us to look hard at the past and,
through reflection, to make the right decisions in
order that the ghosts of the past fade away and we
can create for ourselves lives cleared of the errors
of past actions.

Fire ✦ Yin

PROVERB

Try to steal a chicken and it'll eat your grain while you're
not watching.

The king said, 'Oh, such people!
You are like locusts, like cicadas,
Like boiling water,
Like an over-heated pot
Small and great you bring to ruin.
Men long to do the right thing
But you burn throughout China
Right through to the border!'

MEDITATION

Fire and yin are in conflict. They are locked in a great
struggle. The result is chaos, deception and destruction.
Be careful. The powers swirling around you are awesome.
Act only with caution.

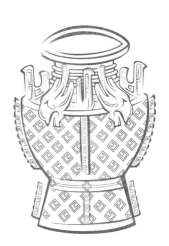

34

fire ◆ Yang

PROVERB

Get your ears pierced before the wedding starts.

When he takes wood for the fire
A man must use an axe!
When a man needs a wife,
He needs a match-maker!
But once he has got her,
He can't burn for anyone else.

MEDITATION

Let everything have its own right time. This teasing poem makes a blunt point. The time for flirting and for making yourself attractive is before commitment of marriage; thereafter, the external is less important than the internal. So it is with all aspects of our life.

fire ◆ Water

PROVERB

A thousand ants can eat a bone.

Drought blights everything —
The hills are parched, and the streams dry.
It holds the land in a tight grasp,
As if scattering fire and flames.
My heart fears the heat —
My tears are on fire.
The wise ones of the past
Speak nothing to me.
O gods, from the heavens
Grant me grace to retire!

MEDITATION

Sometimes it is not the great things that bring us down. The
proverb shows this. Fire and Water are, of course, in conflict:
yin and yang. When we find that events have overwhelmed us,
panic can set in. But step back, seek help from God: take
time and, just as each tiny drop of rain will finally end the
drought or put out the fire, so you will find that life
becomes more balanced once again.

36

fire ◆ fire

PROVERB

Jade is useless unless worked; a man is useless
unless educated.

Heaven's hand is heavy on us
Do not mock sacred things.
I am ancient, and speak the truth
But you, children, are puffed with pride
My speech may be senile
But you laugh at tragedy,
So your troubles will spread like flame
Until there is no hope left for you.

MEDITATION

Take time and trouble to learn. Listen before you offer
advice. Look before you judge. In the *I Ching*, the oldest
Chinese divination and wisdom book, it speaks of the
stranger, the odd one who breaks into our smug,
content worlds and makes us think again. You may
need to stand back and think more deeply, learn
more humbly, what is really important, or else you may find
yourself consumed – like fire upon fire, which swiftly fails,
for it has nothing of substance to feed upon.

fire ◆ Earth

PROVERB

Only by piling up everybody's wood can you make a bonfire.

Come the seventh month, the fire ebbs
By the ninth, we hand out the coats
First days of the first, hard frost
First days of the second, sharp winds
Without coats or covering
How can one last the winter?
In the third month, they plough
In the fourth month, I go out
With all my family
Picnicking in the south fields
Where the farmers come to celebrate.

MEDITATION

The relationship between the elements of Fire and Earth is a complementary one in Chinese philosophy. Fire creates earth from the dust and ashes it produces. The poem reflects a similar understanding. The heat of fire is contrasted with the coming of winter. Both destroy – or seem to do so. Yet, just as earth arises from the aftermath of fire, so spring emerges from the harshness of winter – here, delightfully expressed as going picnicking! So it is with life. From that which appears hard, cold and destructive, the seeds of the new are born.

38

Fire ◆ Metal

PROVERB

Destroy the bridge after you've crossed it.

The warlord grasped his banner
Brandishing his axe high,
Like a blazing fire
Which no one can restrain.
The three-shooted root
Had nowhere to grow.

火
金

MEDITATION

This is a harsh combination. The poem tells of a warlord who, by his actions, brings destruction – so much so that the crops cannot be planted because the land has been wasted.

Be careful. It may be necessary to let go of all that has been, as the proverb says. Or, you should take care because forces stronger than you are at work.

Tread with caution and mindfulness.

Fire ◆ Wood

PROVERB
Water far away won't quench the thirst you have now.

Quick-spreading flames
Char once-dense woods.
Low-stooping falcon
Bends in for the kill.
I have not yet seen my lord
And my heart is sore.

MEDITATION
Fire consumes wood, just as love – especially unrequited
love, or love for someone far from you –
can consume the lover. There is
nothing more to say.

40

Earth ✦ Tao

PROVERB

Even the best cook can't prepare a meal without rice.

Big rat, big king rat,
Do not gobble our crops!
We slaved three years for you
And you take no notice of us!
But we are going to flee,
To go to that happy land,
A happy land, a happy land,
Where no sad songs are sung!

MEDITATION

Troubles come and sometimes, despite all we do, they
overwhelm us. In China, rats are a plague, but the Chinese
have developed a method for controlling them. They leave
food out for them – but only just enough so the rats do not
over-breed. This usually keeps the problem under control,
but occasionally even this does not work. So with life.

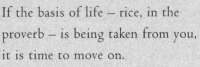

If the basis of life – rice, in the
proverb – is being taken from you,
it is time to move on.

Earth ✦ Yin

PROVERB
Nothing grows in dry earth.

In the middle of the valley
All the herbs are dry.
A lonely girl,
Sobbing bitterly,
Crying harshly,
Faced with man's cruelty.

In the middle of the valley,
The herbs are withered.
A girl alone,
Sighs deeply,
Wails softly,
Faced with man's evil.

土
陰

MEDITATION
Earth is yin, so this is a dry, cold combination. The poem, one of those whose anguish speaks down the millennia, evokes the withering of the soul as well as the withering of the land. When we are dried up, withered, we need to seek the fresh dew of grace, of the spiritual world. Only this can revive dry bones, withered flowers, and help us face the troubles around us.

42

Earth ◆ Yang

土
陽

PROVERB

If you're planning an invasion, build your own fortress first.

They raised the outer walls;
Outer walls, soaring high.
They raised the inner gate;
The inner gate, strong as stone.
They raised the great earth-fortress
When the campaigns began.

MEDITATION

There is little to add to this. Its meaning is clear. Prepare well for any venture; in particular, prepare for failures and disappointments as well as triumphs. Hopefully you will succeed, but if not, then you will be able to survive the disappointments.

PROVERB

Lift too heavy a stone and you'll drop it on your own feet.

The sharp rocks —
Such high rocks!
No end to these hills
Such hard work!
But on the Eastern front
We've no time to stop.

We saw white-trottered pigs —
A herd plunging through the waves.
The net is cast round the moon
Nothing but rain soon.
But on the Eastern front
There's no time to rest.

MEDITATION

The Eastern front refers here to building the Great Wall of China. This vast enterprise took centuries to build, always needing constant maintenance. You have your own Great Wall. When the going gets tough it is tempting either to overdo it, as the proverb says, or to long for escape, as the first part of the second verse of the poem portrays. Find the Middle Way.

44

Earth ◆ Fire

PROVERB

A warm coat is better than a full belly.

Cat resting on the warm roof tiles,
Heat rising up from the fireplace below.
Inside, the farmer snoozes in bed,
No need to move, no need to act at all.

MEDITATION

Earth and Fire complement each other and help create the
very stuff of life itself. This poem is a comforting one in
tone, and is a reminder to be grateful for what you have,
rather than go wandering, searching for that which may
not be so useful.

土
火

Earth ⬧ Earth

PROVERB

If you've never done anything wrong, why worry about devils
knocking on your door?

There's the shaman dancing,
There, on top of the mound,
He may be a man of vision
But he's careless with his name.

Bang; he beats his drum,
Underneath the empty mound
Whether it's winter or summer,
His bird feathers in hand.

MEDITATION

As this poem makes clear, shamans have always been strange
characters, slightly feared. When the spirits possess the
shamans, they cease to worry about how they seem in this
world because they are then in touch with the spiritual
world. All the great spiritual teachers – Zoroaster, Christ,
Muhammad, Guru Nanak, to name a few – were likewise
uninterested in appearing 'normal', for they were touched
or filled by God. Are you?

46

Earth ◆ Metal

PROVERB

Sweat during peace saves blood during war.

Sharp spears thrust into the ground.
This is the border;
This is the marking-place.
No one comes past here.

Watch the guards tremble!
Watch the earth shake!
The warriors are coming,
No fear in their eyes.

MEDITATION

When it seems as if you have done all you can, try once more.
The border is, of course, the Great Wall. At tremendous
cost, China built this barrier in order to prevent
war. As the proverb stresses, extra effort now
to find a solution will prevent the situation
escalating out of control.

47

Earth ◆ Wood

PROVERB

You can't find ivory in a dog's mouth.

The mulberry is up on the mountain
The lotuses are in the marsh
I cannot see my lord
Only this mad man.

The pine grows high on the mountain
Flowers grow on marshy water
I cannot see my lord
Only a crafty boy.

MEDITATION

What is real? The poem contrasts aspects of reality – bushes and trees on mountains, lotus in the marsh – with the vacuousness of the man. Can you tell what is real, or are you looking for ivory in a dog's mouth?

48

Metal ◆ Tao

PROVERB

Sacrificing your conscience to ambition is like burning a painting to get the ashes.

No act of power goes without its reward.
A good deed brings back good in return.
Be gracious, my child, in your power
And bless the common people,
So that your reign may continue forever.

MEDITATION

Is there much to add? Act justly, live humbly and walk quietly with your God.

Metal ✦ Yin

PROVERB

A brother's hatred is worse than twenty sworn enemies.

Soft and pliant the long bow.
It springs back with all speed,
Sends its sharp arrows deep.
Such is the hard pain
Of my kinsmen's absence.

MEDITATION

The clang of metal – yang with yin – fills this poem and
proverb. Anger, violence and jealousy are like arrows into the
soul. Turn instead to the yin – the compassionate – and find
there that which lasts.

50

Metal ◆ Yang

PROVERB

It is the beautiful bird that gets caged.

As a halberd, plumed with feathers,
As an arrow, piercing sharply,
As a bird, soaring into the clouds,
As wings, flying powerfully,
Are the halls to which our lord climbs.

金
陽

MEDITATION

Think not just of this life, where the material aspects are often little more than a trap. Aspire instead to the world beyond – to Heaven. All that is of this world perishes. Only the spirit lives on.

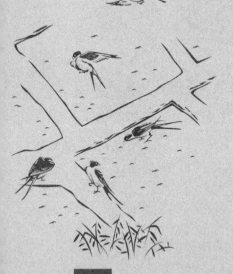

Metal ◆ Water

PROVERB

Kill one, warn a hundred.

Men from all the seas came to pay tribute,
Brought gold and silver and treasures.
Came in great crowds altogether,
Piled up their wealth for the king.

MEDITATION

China, which means 'middle' or 'central' country, saw itself as
the centre of the universe. It expected all other countries to
bring it tribute. It ruled sternly. Sometimes this is necessary,
but a gentle approach should follow.

52

Metal ✦ Fire

PROVERB

A gem can't be worked without friction; a man won't be
perfected without trials.

Watch the smith with his hammer
Crashing it down;
Watch the hammer strike the anvil
Forging the bronze;
Watch the bronze cool and shape
Becoming the armour.

MEDITATION

What we are, what we can become, is forged in the heat and
struggle of life. From the combination of metal and fire can
come artists' wonderful creations — beautiful statues, bronze
mirrors, or even weapons. Struggle and difficulty are not to
be avoided or resented, for they help us to *become*.

金
火

Metal ❖ Earth

PROVERB

Better a tough horse than a swift one.

Tall and strong our stallions,
Bound in the meadow.
See their muscles ripple,
Watch their hooves clash.
War-horses for the king
Oh, pray that forever,
We may have horses this good!

MEDITATION

The world you create around you – can it carry you? Will it
support you in times of difficulty? Like a strong horse, you
need to build a world of family and friends who will prove
true when the time of testing comes, as come it will.

54

Metal ✦ Metal

PROVERB

A spear at your front is better than an arrow in your back.

The armoured team moves in smooth harmony
Brandishing their bright-gilded spears
And their beautiful feathered shields;
With the tiger-skin quivers, and the metal
  decorations in front
Two bows lying side by side
Tied to their bamboo frames.
I think of my absent husband
When I lie down and get up
When will I know when he comes back?
Oh! How I think of him!

金
金

MEDITATION

Metal and Metal is a powerful yang combination. The proverb captures that. The poem, however, brings a yin dimension. Following the celebration of armies and arms, we suddenly hear the voice of a wife, a lover. It breaks in and recalls us to the truth that violence destroys, but love and compassion nurture.

Metal ◆ Wood

PROVERB

When planting for a year, plant corn. A decade, trees.
A century, people.

Chopping for firewood,
Slice the trees up!
Chopping down old trees,
Planting in new.

MEDITATION

Plan ahead, not just for now. There is an old Jewish saying:
'If you are planting a tree and someone comes running to
you saying "The Messiah has come," first finish planting
the tree, then go and see the Messiah.' Prepare a better
world – not necessarily one you will see, but one that future
generations will.

56

Wood ✦ Tao

木道

PROVERB

Tall trees get cut down first.

Streams flow deep down,
Deep down from the south.
May you be as firm as bamboo
As tall as the highest pine
May elder and younger
Always love each other.
Never do evil to each other.

MEDITATION

Wood and Tao: both grow and spread in the right conditions.
This is a good poem, an affirming poem. Be true, be modest
(listen to the proverb) and you will be nurtured by the Tao
as wood is nurtured.

57

Wood ✷ Yin

PROVERB

Not every peach gives immortality.

The peach tree is heavy with fruit
How its flowers shine out!
Our mistress coming home
Brings good times for all of us.

MEDITATION

In Chinese mythology, there is a peach tree in the Celestial
Mountains ruled by the shaman/Taoist goddess, the
Queen Mother of the West. These peaches, if eaten, give
immortality. Most peaches just give pleasure and delight by
their tastiness. Enjoy what is truly within your reach, rather
than hankering after what is honestly beyond you.

58

Wood ◆ Yang

PROVERB

Lost your horse? He might bring a whole herd back to you.

Here we will stop, here we shall stay,
Here in the deep woods.
Here we lose horses, find them again,
Here down in the deep woods.

MEDITATION

Cast your bread upon the waters, says the Bible, and it will come back to you a hundredfold. Sometimes you need to let go in order to truly have what you want.

Wood ✦ Water

PROVERB

A young man wants women, an old man wants rice.

Trees without branches
offer no shelter.
The girls by the river
offer no comfort.

The Han is so deep
you cannot dive it.
The Kiang is so long
you cannot swim it.

I would strip the thorns
From the firewood
I would offer food
To the girls' horses.

MEDITATION

Be content with what you have, just as trees are content to
grow beside streams, nourished by the constant flow of water.

60

Wood ✦ fire

PROVERB

Everything has its beauty, but not everyone can see it.

Along the banks of the river
I cut down the tree-branches.
While I couldn't see my lord
My heart hungered for him.

Along these raised banks
I cut down the slender twigs.
I have seen my lord;
He did not cast me out.

MEDITATION

Look carefully at what it is that you desire. From a distance it can seem so attractive. If, when you draw closer, it is still as desirable, you will know it is right for you. Do not hurry. Take your time.

Wood ◆ Earth

PROVERB

An unreachable well is no use to anybody.

The thick oaks grow on the mountain
Elm trees cling to the marshes.
Without my husband in sight
My heart is without joy.
Why is it, how is it
That he has forgotten me?

The plums bloom on the mountain
Pear trees spring on the marshes.
Without my husband in sight
My heart cries with grief.
Why is it, how is it
That he has forgotten me?

MEDITATION

Are you longing for the unachievable? Is it perhaps time
to wake up and realize things have changed and
you should move on?

木
土

62

Wood ◆ Metal

PROVERB

Better to pay your tax than have your head cut off.

The owls come flying on the wing,
Settling on the trees about the college.
They strip the fruit from the mulberries
And greet us with their songs.

That should wake up the southern tribes
They will come with their tribute
Great tortoise-shells and ivory tusks
And all their precious metals.

MEDITATION

Just as spring heralds the coming of summer, and the
southern tribes brought tribute to the Emperor of China, so
you may need to give thanks for all the good things in life.
Offer to those who love you, to God and to the world,
your gratitude for life itself.

63

Wood ✦ Wood

PROVERB

Only cracked eggs draw flies.

Even the flood-waters
Will not carry off well-bound wood
You and I are together
As long as life lasts.
Do not believe the rumours;
They are nothing but lies.

Even the flood-waters
Will not carry off well-bound wood
We two are kin
As long as life lasts.
Do not believe people's lies;
They are simply not to be trusted.

MEDITATION

If there is truth, nothing can break it: not rumours,
nor lies. If there is falsehood – the cracked egg of
the proverb – then it will soon become apparent.

64

further Reading

PLEASE NOTE: Books are listed with the first date of publication, and were in print at the time of going to press.

The Book of Songs, Arthur Waley. First publication 1947/Grove Press reprint, 1996

Chinese Mythology, Anne Birrell. Baltimore: John Hopkins University Press, 1993

Essential Chinese Mythology, Martin Palmer and Zhao Xiaomin. London: Thorsons, 1996

A History of Chinese Philosophy, Vol. 1, Fung Yu-lan. Princeton University Press, 1952

I Ching, Martin Palmer, Jay Ramsay and Man-Ho Kwok. London: Thorsons, 1995

Ling Ch'i Ching, Ralph D. Sawyer and Mei-ch'un Lee Sawyer. Boston: Shambala, 1995

'She King' in *Sacred Books of the East*, James Legge and Max Muller (ed.). Oxford University Press, 1989

Sources of Chinese Tradition, Theodore de Bary. New York: Columbia University Press, 1960

Acknowledgements

AUTHORS' ACKNOWLEDGEMENTS

We wish to express our deepest gratitude to James Palmer, Martin's son, who spent days working on the repoeticization of our terrible translations and who brought to this task his own profound understanding of the world of Chinese divination, soothsaying, humour, mythology and wit. Martin also wishes to thank Jeannie Dunn and Gena Darwent who helped with so many practical aspects of this book, while Xiaomin wishes to thank his daughter for having slept through some of the more difficult bits of this project!

We both owe a continuing debt of gratitude to the many Taoist priests who, over the years, have shared with us their insights, their wisdom and their knowledge. In particular, Master Hun Tzu, Grand Master Liu, Vice Secretary Zhang and, of course, Master Kon Yiu. To all of them, we offer our thanks for days of discussion and years of knowledge so gladly shared and so openly enjoyed.

Martin Palmer and Zhao Xiaomin.

EDDISON • SADD EDITIONS

EDITORIAL DIRECTOR Ian Jackson
SENIOR EDITOR Tessa Monina
PROOFREADER Nikky Twyman

PRODUCTION Karyn Claridge and Charles James

ART DIRECTOR Elaine Partington
SENIOR ART EDITOR Pritty Ramjee
DESIGNER Malcolm Smythe

ILLUSTRATIONS Colin Brown/Beehive Illustration and Jon Meakin

道
道

1
Tao ✦ Tao
(page 16)

道
陰

2
Tao ✦ Yin
(page 17)

道
陽

3
Tao ✦ Yang
(page 18)

道
水

4
Tao ✦ Water
(page 19)

道
火

5
Tao ✦ Fire
(page 20)

道
土

6
Tao ✦ Earth
(page 21)

道
金

7
Tao ✦ Metal
(page 22)

道
木

8
Tao ✦ Wood
(page 23)

陰
道

9
Yin ✦ Tao
(page 24)

陰
陰

10
Yin ✦ Yin
(page 25)

陰
陽

11
Yin ✦ Yang
(page 26)

陰
水

12
Yin ✦ Water
(page 27)

陰
火

13
Yin ✦ Fire
(page 28)

陰
土

14
Yin ✦ Earth
(page 29)

陰
金

15
Yin ✦ Metal
(page 30)

陰
木

16
Yin ✦ Wood
(page 31)

陽
道

17
Yang ✦ Tao
(page 32)

陽
陰

18
Yang ✦ Yin
(page 33)

陽
陽

19
Yang ✦ Yang
(page 34)

陽
水

20
Yang ✦ Water
(page 35)

陽
火

21
Yang ✦ Fire
(page 36)

陽
土

22
Yang ✦ Earth
(page 37)

陽
金

23
Yang ✦ Metal
(page 38)

陽
木

24
Yang ✦ Wood
(page 39)

水
道

25
Water ✦ Tao
(page 40)

水
陰

26
Water ✦ Yin
(page 41)

水
陽

27
Water ✦ Yang
(page 42)

水
水

28
Water ✦ Water
(page 43)

水
火

29
Water ✦ Fire
(page 44)

水
土

30
Water ✦ Earth
(page 45)

水
金

31
Water ✦ Metal
(page 46)

水
木

32
Water ✦ Wood
(page 47)